First edition published in 2024 by Flying Eye Books Ltd.
27 Westgate Street, London, E8 3RL.

Illustrations © Ben Newman 2024

Scientific consultant: Gill Perkins

1 3 5 7 9 10 8 6 4 2

Text by Ben Elcomb
Edited by Sara Forster
Designed by Sarah Crookes

Published in the US by Flying Eye Books Ltd.

Printed in China on FSC® certified paper.

ISBN: 978-1-838748-58-6

www.flyingeyebooks.com

THE BEE CONNECTION

BEN NEWMAN

FLYING EYE BOOKS

CONTENTS

WELCOME TO STEMVILLE

You've stumbled across one of the most amazing places there is to visit. Stemville is home to lots of weird and wonderful characters of all shapes and sizes. Most of the time the residents get along just fine, but occasionally sparks fly and there are disagreements and problems to solve. One thing's for sure, there's always something new to discover in this terrific town!

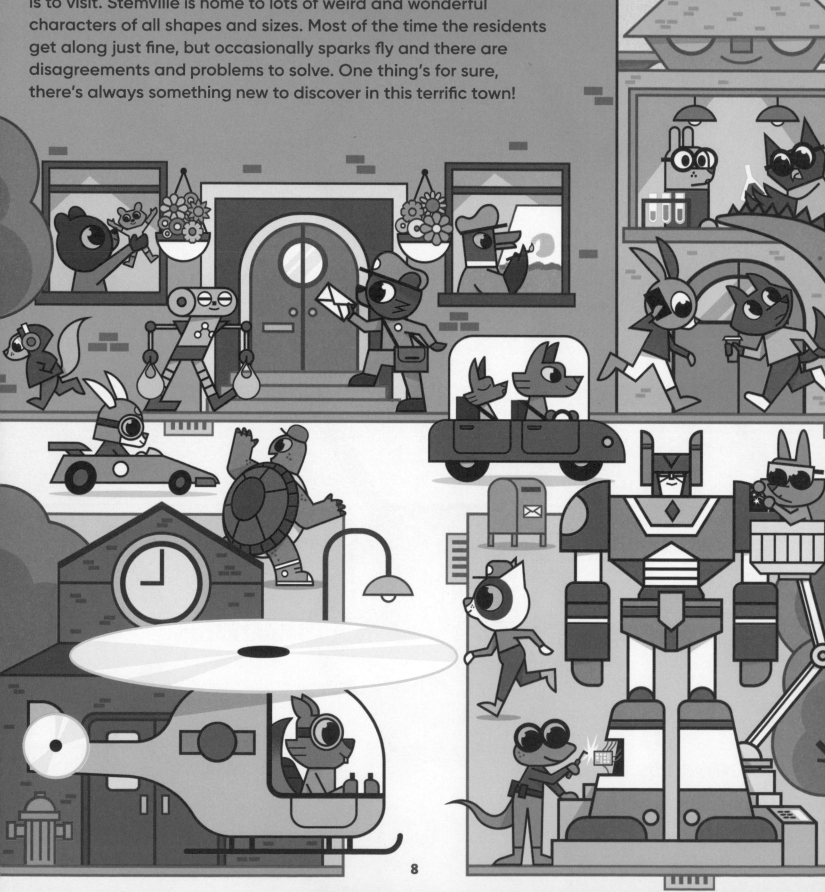

BUG BOROUGH

Bug Borough is home to some of Stemville's smallest residents! Any insect, minuscule or mighty, is welcome here and it's a busy place to be. Look closely and you'll spot everyone going about their day-to-day lives. There's a new business in town that's creating a bit of buzz . . . a private detective agency. Just wait till you meet street-smart Mason B. Chandler; she's a solitary bee on a mission. If there's a mystery to be solved in Bug Borough, then Mason is your bee.

Here are a few handy clues to help you identify an insect: Most insects have six legs, two pairs of wings, antennae, and a body that has three sections.

Beetles *have a hard shell to protect their wings.*

Ants *have long antennae that bend in the middle, just like elbows on your arms.*

So, What Is an Insect?

Insects are invertebrates—small animals that don't have a backbone. Insects don't have bones inside their bodies. Instead, they have a hard shell called an exoskeleton. 75% of all animals on Earth are insects and they come in many shapes and sizes.

Mosquitoes have long, narrow wings and their front legs point forward.

Praying mantises have triangular-shaped heads and very large eyes.

Hoverflies have large round eyes, short antennae, and a single pair of wings.

I'M JUST BUZZING FOR MY FIRST CASE!

DETECTIVE
AGENCY

Bees have two pairs of wings that they can beat up to 200 times per second.

Wasps have narrow waists and two pairs of wings.

Ladybugs have domed-shaped bodies and brightly colored wing covers to tell predators "I don't taste nice."

11

MASON BEES

Meet Mason B. Chandler, solitary bee and proprietor of the Mason B. Chandler Detective Agency! Mason is a friendly and inquisitive bee by nature, who gets along with everyone she meets. However, like other solitary bees, Mason prefers her own company, so this new office is her perfect working-from-home space.

There are over 20,000 known species of bees, and they are divided into three groups: honeybees, bumblebees, and solitary bees. While some species, like honeybees and bumblebees, live in a group called a colony, more than 90% of bees are solitary, including mason bees.

Mason Bee Anatomy

Like all insects, bees have a hard outer shell called an exoskeleton. A bee's body is divided into three main parts: a head, a thorax, and an abdomen. The thorax is the middle section of the body, where two pairs of wings and three pairs of legs are attached. At the front of their head, bees have a pair of antennae that they use to detect sounds and scents.

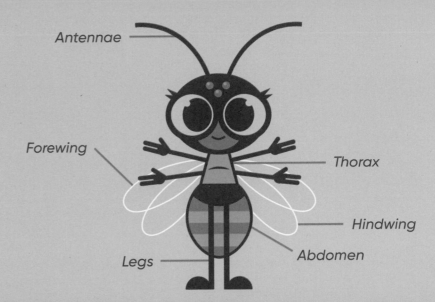

Antennae

Forewing

Thorax

Hindwing

Abdomen

Legs

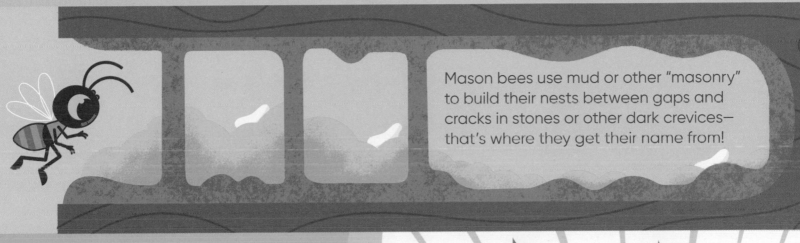

Mason bees use mud or other "masonry" to build their nests between gaps and cracks in stones or other dark crevices—that's where they get their name from!

Things have got off to a slow start for Mason's detective agency. With so much activity going on around her she had expected things to be a little livelier. Surely it won't be long before her first case lands on her desk with a . . .

CRASH!

WHO IS HONEY?

Bug Borough has come to a standstill. A golden, oozy substance is everywhere, causing quite a commotion, with residents of Bug Borough getting stuck! Taking her cue from the Bug Police, Mason tastes the sticky goo. It's delicious and sweet, and she instantly feels energized. If she's not mistaken, it's honey! But how did it end up all over Stemville?

Among the chaos, Mason spots a clue. There's a label on the jar and as she takes a closer look, she's shocked to see a picture of a bee that looks just like her . . . except it can't be! Mason is a solitary bee and doesn't make honey. She doesn't know much about honey but maybe her friends in the solitary bee apartments might be able to help . . .

Is that a bee hovering above? Perhaps another private detective trying to solve the case? A closer look reveals it's actually Hoverfly—an easy mistake to make.

Mason also spies a group of wasps. If there is one thing Mason knows about wasps, it's that they love anything sweet.

Honey tastes sweet because it is about 80% sugar and 20% water.

Eating a small amount of honey can help you stay healthy and fight disease. Honey can also help with digestion.

Honey contains a lot of sugar though, so eating too much can cause tooth decay and obesity.

Honey never goes out of date! A jar of honey survived from ancient Egypt. After thousands of years it was still good to eat.

SOLITARY APARTMENTS

At the Solitary Apartments, Mason fills her neighbors in on the case. When Mason mentions that the honey was sweet, one of the bees thinks that this could be because honey contains nectar. Nectar is the sugar-rich liquid that plants produce, making them irresistibly tasty! Mason decides it's time to find some flowers . . . this could be just the lead she needs to crack the case!

There's that hoverfly again, even he has an apartment here.

I GET THE FEELING I'M BEE-ING WATCHED . . .

As their name suggests, solitary bees live on their own and don't belong to a colony.

16

Meet the Neighbors

There are lots of different types of solitary bee (including mason bees) but here are the three main types:

Mining bees *are ground-nesting solitary bees between 5-17 mm. in size. They often leave volcano-shaped piles of soil at the entrance to their nests.*

Carpenter bees *like to tunnel into wood to create their nests. They create their nest tunnel by chewing wood with their strong jaws.*

Leaf-cutting bees *use sections of leaves to make their nests. The female bee uses her jaws to cut small circular pieces from plant leaves.*

Nest Builders

All solitary bee nests are built by female bees. They build their nests in hollow stalks or in soil, sand, clay, mortar, or wood. Most solitary bees nest on their own, but in ideal sites you can sometimes find clusters of nests.

Nesting Chamber of a Mining Bee

1. First, the female mining bee collects building materials for her nest and food for her larvae.

2. Then she finds a suitable piece of ground in which to build her nest and digs out a nesting chamber.

3. She fills each chamber with pollen, often moistened by nectar, which will act as a food supply for her offspring when they hatch.

4. Finally, she lays an egg, before sealing off that section and moving on to the next one.

POLLINATION

Mason arrives at a beautiful flower meadow. In the bright sunshine, it is alive with the buzz of busy bees doing what they do best: visiting flower after flower, feasting on sweet nectar and picking up pollen along the way. Mason spots so many different types of bees, how will she ever find the bee from the label?

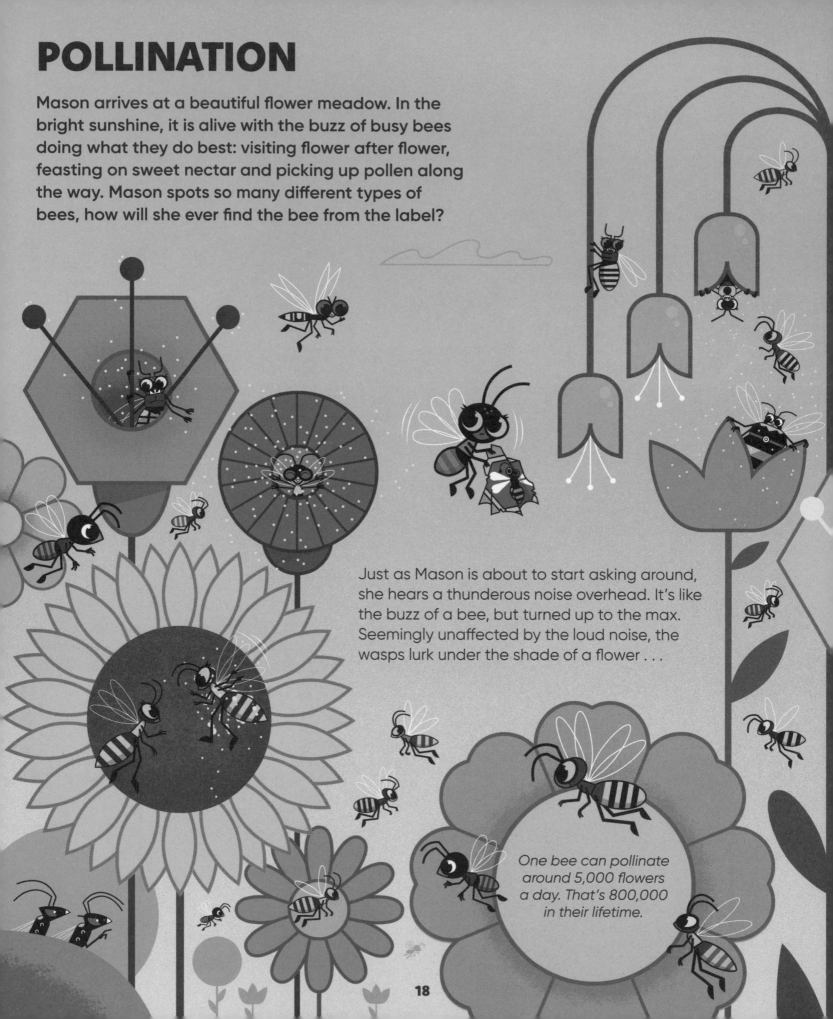

Just as Mason is about to start asking around, she hears a thunderous noise overhead. It's like the buzz of a bee, but turned up to the max. Seemingly unaffected by the loud noise, the wasps lurk under the shade of a flower . . .

One bee can pollinate around 5,000 flowers a day. That's 800,000 in their lifetime.

Pollination Station

Bees make excellent pollinators because they have furry legs and bodies. As the bee visits the flower, pollen catches onto the fur and can then be transported with the bee.

Anther

1
The bright color of flower petals and a sweet smell tell bees, and other pollinating insects like hoverflies, that the flower has sugary nectar.

2
The bee enjoys the flower's sweet nectar with its long, strawlike tongue, called a proboscis. Tiny dustlike pollen grains, produced by the part of the flower called the anther, get stuck to the bee.

Pollen grains

Stigma

3
When the bee visits another flower, the pollen is transferred to the sticky part, called the stigma, on this new flower. This is when pollination occurs meaning the plant can now produce fruit and seeds, which will in turn grow into new plants.

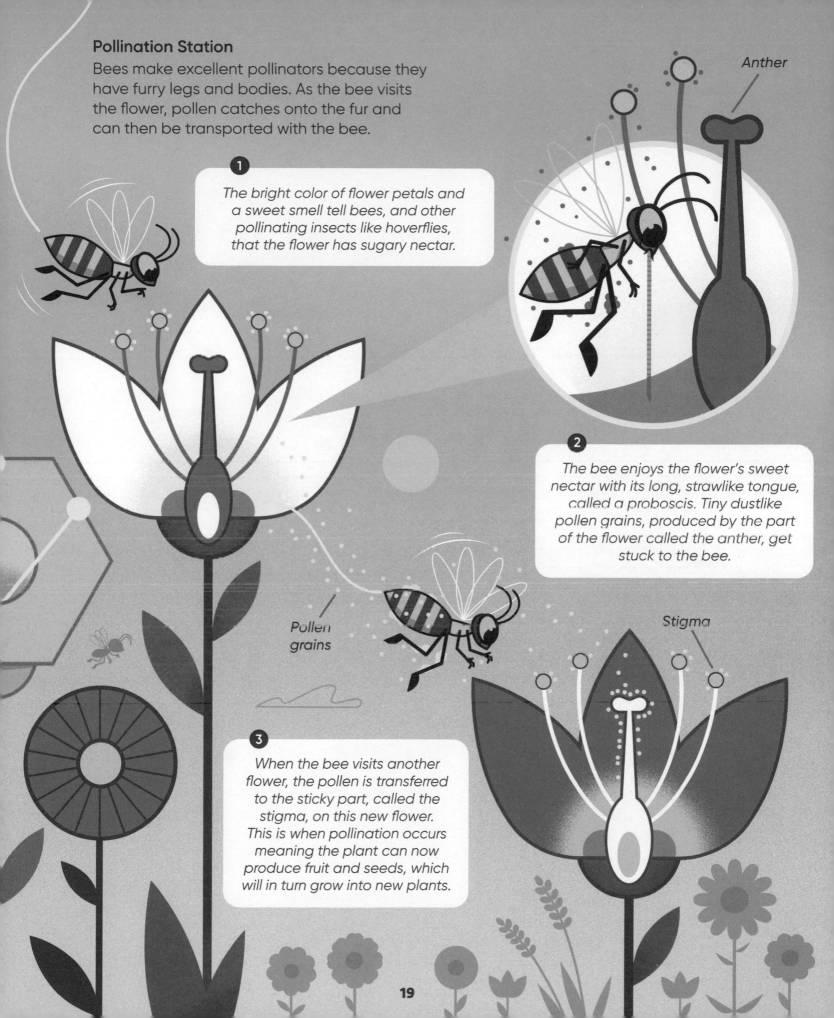

BUMBLEBEES

When the loud buzzing stops, Mason finds herself next to a large, furry bee who's twice her size. The newcomer introduces herself as Bumble, the bumblebee.

Mason asks Bumble whether she knows anything about honey. Just like mason bees, bumblebees don't make honey either, but Bumble reckons if they follow the bees who are leaving the meadow, they are sure to find the honey-making hub.

Bumblebees have four wings that can beat up to 240 times per second. The buzzing sound a bumblebee makes is caused by the muscles in its thorax vibrating.

When a bumblebee approaches a flower, the vibration of its flight muscles causes the flower to spill pollen over the bumblebee. This is called buzz pollination.

Bumblebees are the largest species of bee and are fluffy in appearance. Their hairy bodies help keep them warm in colder climates and makes them excellent pollinators.

Bumblebees can grow up to 4 cm. in length and weigh up to 0.5 oz.

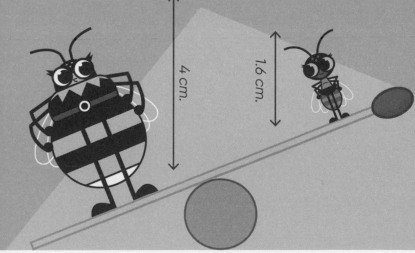

Mason bees can grow up to 1.6 cm. in length and weigh up to .003 oz.

THE SWEET VALLEY HIVES

Mason and Bumble arrive at Sweet Valley Hives. Mason thinks it all looks a bit chaotic with bees coming and going all the time. They also appear to be performing some kind of random dance. Bumble points out that if you look closely, you'll notice it's not just any dance, it's the waggle dance—the dance that bees returning to the hive use to let other bees know where they collected the very best pollen.

It's time for Bumble to work her magic and get them into the hive so they can find out where the bees are taking the pollen . . .

Dancing Bees

Bees have a clever way of sharing the location of particularly good flower patches with other members of their hive. When a bee returns to the hive, it smells like the flower patch it has visited and will often share a taste of the nectar it found there. The smell and taste of the nectar will help the other bees to identify the right patch. Then, she performs one of two special dances to give the other bees directions.

The waggle dance tells watching bees the distance between the hive and the flower patch, as well as the direction to go in.

Bees move forward in a straight line, then circle around to repeat the dance.

The length of the middle line, called the waggle run, shows how far away the patch is.

A one-second run indicates the flowers are roughly 2/3 of a mile away.

The circle dance is thought to let other bees know that the flower patch is close to the hive, but no more detail than that.

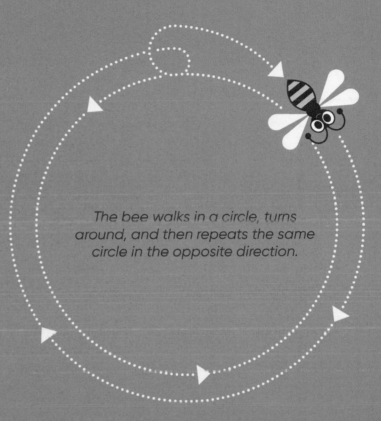

The bee walks in a circle, turns around, and then repeats the same circle in the opposite direction.

The bee often waggles as she turns to reverse the circle. The duration of this waggle is thought to indicate the quality of the flower patch.

THIS BEE KNOWS HOW TO BOOGIE!

WORKER AND DRONE HONEYBEES

Mason and Bumble meet a very busy bee called Honey who explains that females like herself are called worker bees. As well as collecting pollen and nectar outside, worker bees are responsible for all the housekeeping inside the hive too, including making enough honey to feed every bee in the hive.

Caught up with the wasps, the hive guards don't notice Hoverfly sauntering in.

The majority of bees in a hive are worker bees. An average hive will have 20,000-80,000 worker bees, 500 drones, and one queen bee.

Each colony starts the season in spring with about 10,000-15,000 bees. By the summer, this will have risen to around 50,000-80,000 bees.

Honey points to a group of male bees, called drones, who don't look quite so busy. However, Honey will need the queen bee's permission to show Mason and Bumble any more of the hive.

Honeybee Anatomy

Worker bees are female.

Bees have five eyes. They have three smaller eyes that detect light and help them to locate pollen, and two larger eyes to help the bee to see in front, to the side, above, and below.

Like all bees, a worker bee has a pair of antennae. They use their antennae to communicate and detect smells.

A honeybee flies at about 15 mph, with its wings beating 200 times per second.

Worker bees have a group of hairs on their back legs called a "pollen basket." The bees collect pollen, which they have moistened with saliva, and pack it into their pollen baskets to carry back to their hive.

Honeybees have a distinctive stripy body.

Worker bees have a barbed stinger.

Drone bees are male.

Drones have a rounder head.

A drone bee has a pair of antennae.

A drone bee's eyes are twice as big as a worker bee's eyes. They need big eyes to be able to spot the queen bee.

Drones have strong flight muscles that help them chase after the queen bee. They must compete with hundreds or even thousands of other drones to mate with the queen.

Drones have a shorter, wider abdomen and large wings.

A drone bee's only job is to mate with the queen bee, so they don't have a pollen basket.

Male bees do not have a stinger.

THE QUEEN HONEYBEE

Honey has managed to secure Mason and Bumble an audience with a Very Important Bee, Queenie, the queen bee. Mason notices that Queenie is a little bigger than Honey, and definitely not as active. The queen sits on her throne, with her ladies-in-waiting beside her ready to groom and feed her.

Queenie welcomes Mason and Bumble to the hive and listens with interest about their investigation so far. She suggests that maybe one of the hive's nursery bees might be able to help them discover more answers.

A queen bee produces all the eggs in the hive. In the spring, she will lay over 2,000 per day. That's about one egg every twenty seconds, and more than her own body weight in eggs each day. Each egg is about 1.7 mm. long and 0.4 mm. wide.

Actual size

The queen lays fertilized and unfertilized eggs. Fertilized eggs will become worker bees or a future queen bee and unfertilized eggs will become drones.

A hive can only have one queen bee. When a new queen hatches, she uses her stinger to kill any unhatched queens. If two new queens hatch at the same time, they will fight to the death.

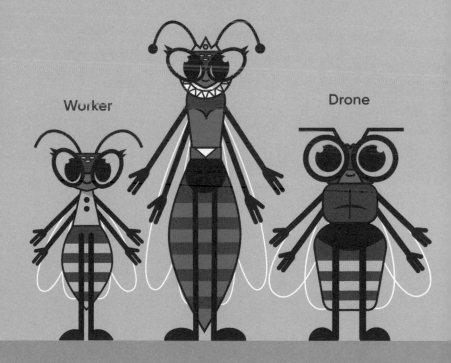

Worker   Queen   Drone

The queen bee has a much longer abdomen than other bees, making her the largest bee in the colony. She also has a hairless, shiny black back and longer legs.

LIFE ON THE HONEYCOMB

Mason and Bumble find themselves in a very busy nursery school. One of the workers explains that for the first few days the youngest bees are fed a jellylike baby food, then a honey and pollen mixture for a few days, before they take an extended nap that lasts for about two weeks. After this, they are ready to take up their adult duties.

Mason realizes how important honey is to the whole hive. These bees wouldn't be so wasteful as to spill it all over Bug Borough . . . so who did?

Three days after an egg is laid it turns into a larva. A larva is a tiny white grub that sheds its skin five times as it grows and consumes 1,300 meals a day.

When the larva has grown to 1,570 times its original size, the worker bees seal it in an individual cell using beeswax in a process called capping.

The Life Cycle of a Bee

All honeybees develop in four distinct life cycle phases— egg, larva, pupa, and adult.

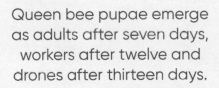

Queen bee pupae emerge as adults after seven days, workers after twelve and drones after thirteen days.

Inside its sealed cell, the young bee is now known as a pupa and begins to transform with familiar bee eyes, legs, and wings taking shape.

The adult bee chews through the beeswax when it is ready to emerge and joins the other bees in the hive.

WHO'S WHO IN THE HIVE?

As a bee who is used to living on her own, Mason is amazed at how thousands of bees manage to live in such perfect harmony. Honey explains that the hive runs so smoothly because each bee is tasked with particular chores, helping to keep the hive running like clockwork.

Nursing
Nursing bees are responsible for feeding and caring for the larvae before they develop into bees during thirteen days of dormancy.

Attending the Queen
The queen has a group of bees dedicated to grooming and feeding her.

Hive Cleaning
There are worker bees who regularly clean out the cells and get rid of any debris in the hive.

Bee Cleaning
Other bees provide a cleaning service for fellow bees, working quickly to remove dust, stray hairs, and anything else that shouldn't be on them.

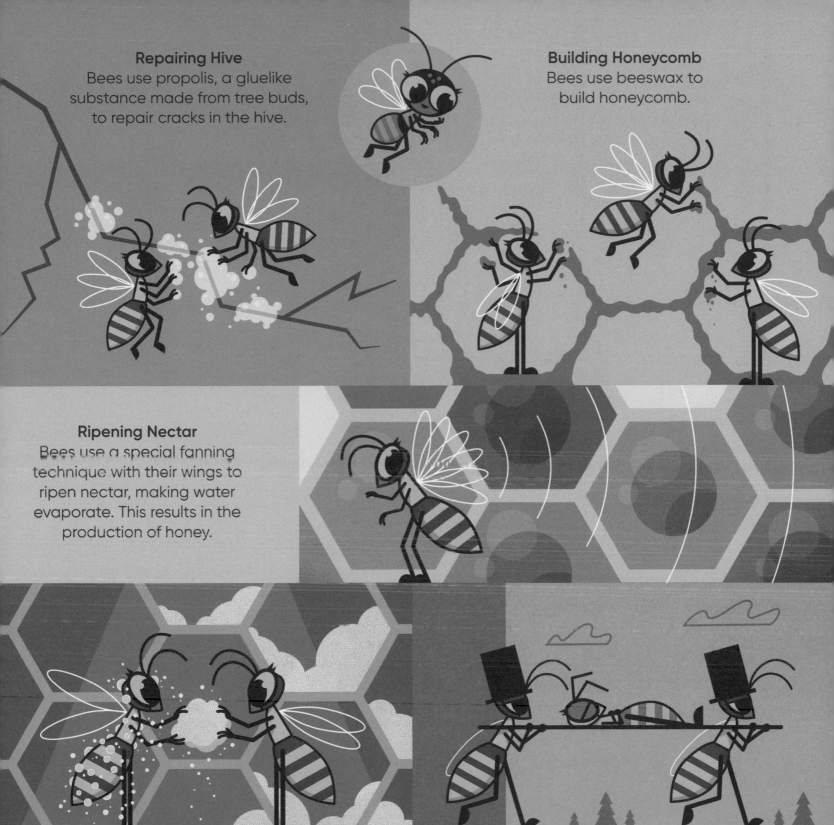

Repairing Hive
Bees use propolis, a gluelike substance made from tree buds, to repair cracks in the hive.

Building Honeycomb
Bees use beeswax to build honeycomb.

Ripening Nectar
Bees use a special fanning technique with their wings to ripen nectar, making water evaporate. This results in the production of honey.

Pollen Packing
Other bees are responsible for collecting pollen from returning foragers and packing it in cells to be eaten later.

Undertaking
Around 90% of bees die outside the hive, but there are undertaker bees on hand to remove any who die inside the hive walls.

INCREDIBLE STRUCTURES

Since entering the hive, Mason has been struck by its impressive architecture; she's never seen anything quite like it. The hexagonal pattern fits together neatly and rigidly, and despite the hive being so busy, there are very few damaged areas.

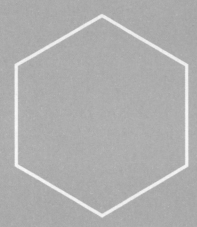

On first inspection, it might appear that honeycomb is made of lots of circles, but if you look closely you'll notice they're actually six-sided hexagons.

Unlike circles, hexagons fit perfectly together without any gaps. When shapes fit perfectly together we call this tessellation.

Hexagons are incredibly strong, using the least amount of material to hold the most amount of weight. Many buildings, bridges, and vehicles have even borrowed this structural shape from nature to strengthen the design.

Bees build hundreds and hundreds of these honeycomb cells, which are packed together to make a nest. Some cells are filled with honey and others will be used by the queen to lay her eggs.

Bees secrete a special substance called beeswax. Hundreds of bees work together using the beeswax to build the honeycomb.

While Mason is admiring the wall of honeycomb, a cloud of smoke starts to descend, filling the hive. Mason begins to panic.

HARVESTING HONEY

Outside the hive, Stemville's resident beekeeper has arrived. He's dressed in his white overalls, boots, gloves, and his all-important hat and veil . . . and he is using his smoker to calm the bees.

Beekeepers use a "smoker" to pump smoke into the hive when collecting honey. A "smoker" consists of a bellow, nozzle, and fire chamber.

The smoke helps to calm the bees and prevents the beekeeper getting stung. It also masks a special smell, called a pheromone, which bees release to alert other bees to danger.

Hat

Veil

Gloves

Jacket

Smoker

Boots

The fear of danger, from the smoke, also makes the bees eat lots of honey . . . just in case they need the energy to fly away and start a new hive. Being full of honey also makes the bees less likely to sting. This is because they feel sluggish, just like we do after a big meal!

Parts of a Beehive

Manufactured hives are essentially a wooden box with a rooflike lid, filled with vertical frames, called honey supers, for bees to deposit their honey.

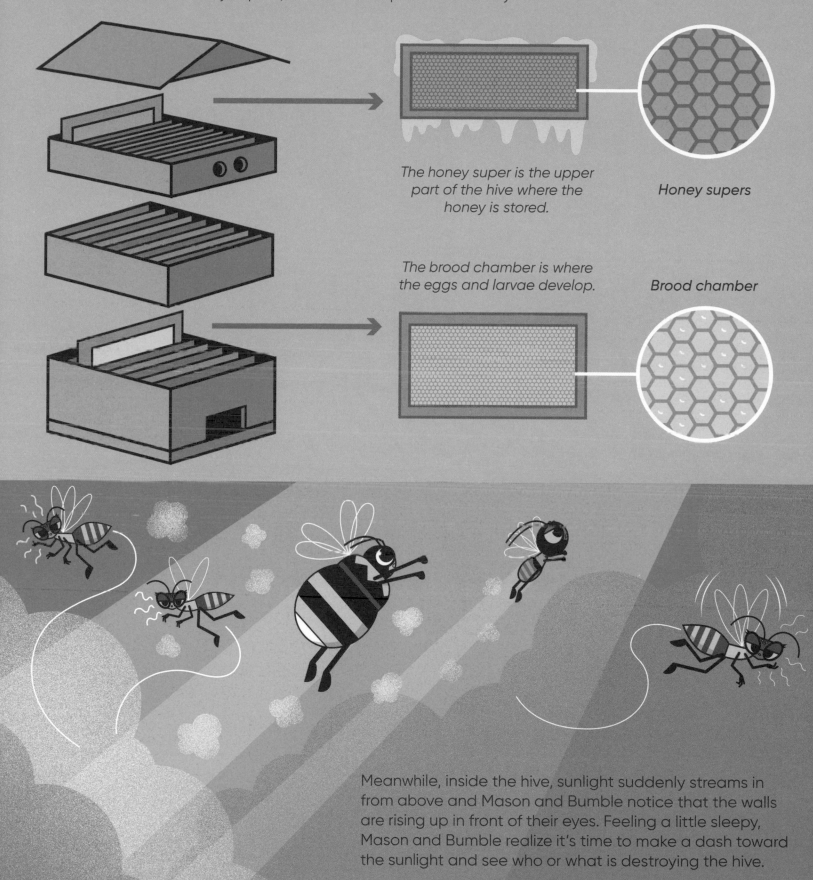

The honey super is the upper part of the hive where the honey is stored.

Honey supers

The brood chamber is where the eggs and larvae develop.

Brood chamber

Meanwhile, inside the hive, sunlight suddenly streams in from above and Mason and Bumble notice that the walls are rising up in front of their eyes. Feeling a little sleepy, Mason and Bumble realize it's time to make a dash toward the sunlight and see who or what is destroying the hive.

WHERE DOES THE HONEY GO?

Mason and Bumble follow the beekeeper back to his home, and to a room filled with jars of honey. They decide to corner this honey thief: they want answers and they want them now!

 The average bee only produces a tiny 1/12th of a teaspoon of honey in its whole lifetime.

Bees produce 2-3 times more honey than they need, meaning beekeepers can collect the excess.

The color and flavor of honey can change depending on the type of flower visited by honeybees.

A single hive can produce between 30-60 pounds of honey a year.

To make around 1 pound of honey, a hive of bees must travel over 55,000 miles and visit 2,000,000 flowers.

Watching over all the action are the scheming wasps. This bee detective and her bumbling sidekick are getting far too close to the truth for their liking . . .

A WORLD WITHOUT BEES

The beekeeper tells Mason and Bumble that he wasn't destroying the hive, he actually helps the honeybees by looking after them and their hive. Bees are vital to the planet's survival; without them, plants wouldn't be pollinated, crops would fail, and people would starve.

The beekeeper says he uses the honey for all sorts of things: healing burns, soothing a sore throat, sweetening tea, and not forgetting his favorite snack—honey on toast!

Convinced she has solved the case, Mason puts it to the beekeeper that if he loves honey so much, why drop a jar over Bug Borough? The beekeeper is about to explain when he spots the wasps and freezes. Without his protective gear on, he's a target for their painful stings . . . and they look angry!

One in every three mouthfuls of food you eat depends on pollinators like bees.

Almost 90% of wild plants depend on animal pollination.

Bees pollinate seventy of the top one hundred food crops we eat.

Broccoli, asparagus, cucumbers, apples, cherries, almonds, and watermelons wouldn't be available without bees pollinating their flowers.

Why Are Bees Disappearing?

Sadly many types of wild bees are in decline around the world. Problems like habitat loss, pollution, harmful chemicals called pesticides, and parasites all affect bees, which is why we need to look out for them.

PREDATORS & DEFENSE

Fearing that he is looking like the bad guy, the beekeeper decides to confess: he did drop the honey over Bug Borough. But it was an accident! He only dropped it because the wasps were menacing him.

The wasps have heard enough and decide to ambush Mason, Bumble, and the beekeeper, and demand all the honey. Despite attempting to use their stingers to defend themselves, it looks like Mason and Bumble are outnumbered.

Hearing the disturbance, Hoverfly appears and checks what's going on.

A Sting in their Tail

Unlike a honeybee's barbed stinger, a wasp's stinger is smooth and does not get stuck in flesh. Wasps can retract their sting into their bodies, meaning they can sting over and over again.

I'M HARMLESS REALLY . . . WELL, MOST OF THE TIME!

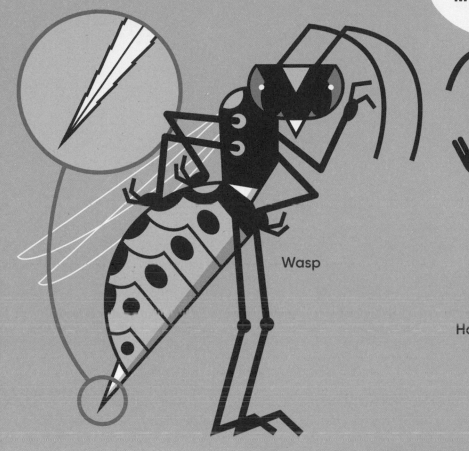

Wasp

Honeybee

Wasps have been known to attack hives to not only eat the honey, but also the pupae and larvae, which they take back to their own carnivorous larvae.

After a honeybee stings it dies because it leaves its stinger and part of its digestive system in the victim. But remember, bees will rarely sting you unless you provoke their hive or accidentally squish one.

HOVERFLY HERO

Just as Mason fears that she won't ever be able to reveal the truth about the villainous wasps to the rest of Stemville, the baddies are covered in sticky honey, leaving them unable to move. How did that happen?

Looking up, Mason sees that helpful Hoverfly has poured a spoonful of honey over the wasps, leaving them in a gloopy prison.

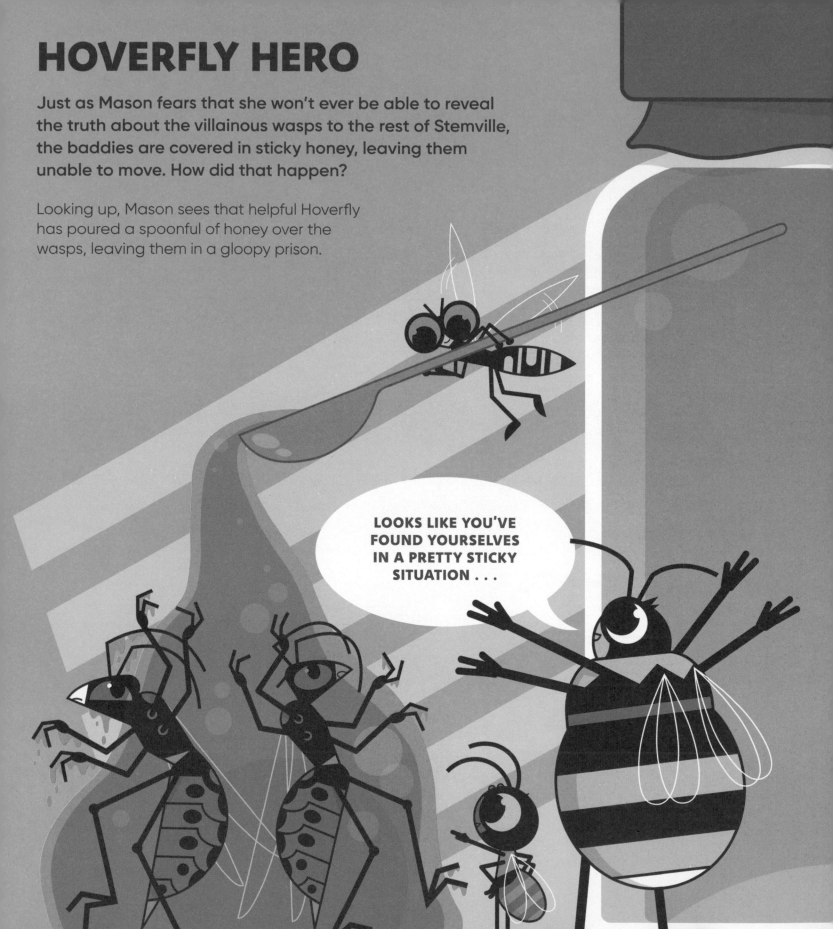

Hoverfly Anatomy

Hoverflies are the second most important pollinators, after wild bees. There are over 6,000 different types of hoverflies.

Hoverflies are true flies.

Even on a windy day, hoverflies are able to fly forward, backward, and hover by constantly adjusting each individual wing pattern and frequency.

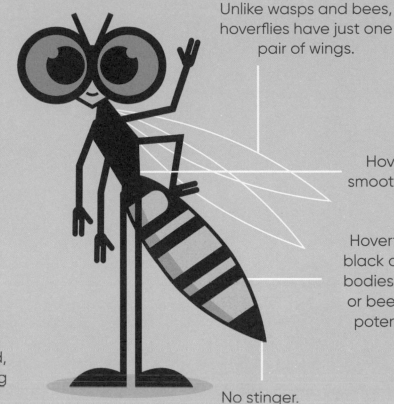

Unlike wasps and bees, hoverflies have just one pair of wings.

Hoverflies have a smooth, hairless body.

Hoverflies often have black and yellow stripy bodies to mimic wasps or bees. This is to trick potential predators.

No stinger.

Slow and Sticky

Viscosity is the property of a liquid that describes how fast or slowly it flows when you pour it. You can think of viscosity as how thick a liquid is.

Honey has a high viscosity so it will flow slowly.

Water has a low viscosity so it will flow quickly.

Honey is sticky because it contains dissolved sugars and some wax. The thick, gooey consistency of honey helps it from dripping or being washed away in the rain.

BYE FOR NOW . . .

As she sits on top of a jar of honey, with her new friends, Bumble and Hoverfly, Mason is feeling pumped that she's solved the case. And better still, they have a perfect bee's eye view of the honey-drenched wasps being carted off by the Bug Police.

Once again, harmony has been restored to Stemville. That is, at least, until the next time . . .

HOW TO BEE FRIENDLY!

Try growing some bee-friendly flowers like marigolds, primroses, sunflowers, or lavender.

Build a bee hotel. Just tie together some hollow bamboo and twigs with string and place it in the bushes or somewhere sheltered.

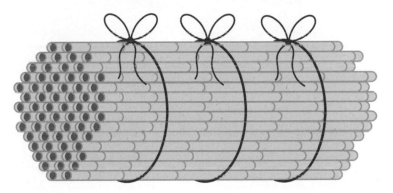

If you come across a tired bee on the ground you can give it a helping hand by very gently placing it on a nearby flower or offering it a spoonful of sugar water. Remember to be very gentle, use a leaf or a piece of paper to carefully move the bee or ask an adult for help.